DANIEL IN THE LION'S DEN

Written by Jane R. Latourette

Illustrated by Sally Mathews

ARCH Books

© 1966 CONCORDIA PUBLISHING HOUSE, ST. LOUIS, MISSOURI

MANUFACTURED IN THE UNITED STATES OF AMERICA

ISBN 0-570-06018-4

Have you heard of Daniel,
a brave Jewish man
whom the king of Ba-by-lon
put into a lions' den?
Why was he punished so?
And what happened then?

Prince Daniel served the king,
who liked him so
it made the other princes mad.
"Let's get rid of him," they said.
"But isn't it too bad
we cannot say old Daniel does
a single thing that's wrong?
We'll have to trick him
some sly way.
We'll watch him all day long."

Now, other men in Ba-by-lon
prayed to a lot of different gods.
But Daniel,
all the long years through,
to our own God was always true.

These jealous men
saw Daniel go
into his room next day.
They listened on the ground below,
as Daniel knelt to pray.

"Aha!" they cried.
"This helps our plan!"
And to the palace these men ran.

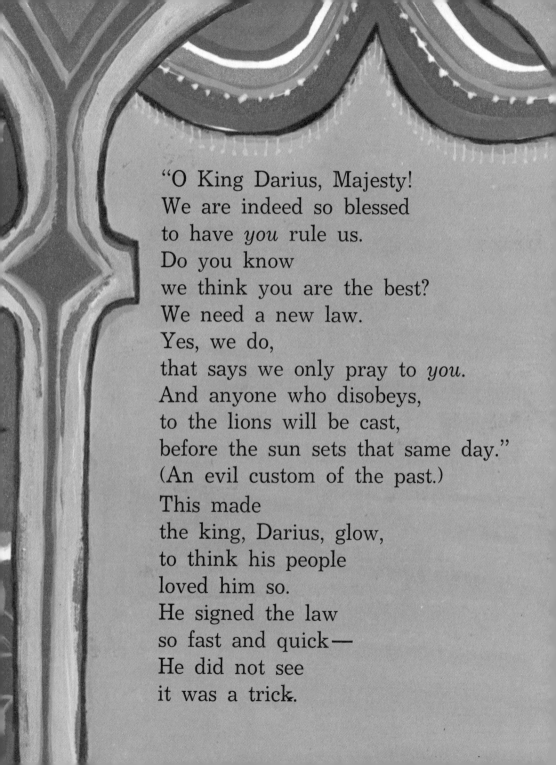

"O King Darius, Majesty!
We are indeed so blessed
to have *you* rule us.
Do you know
we think you are the best?
We need a new law.
Yes, we do,
that says we only pray to *you*.
And anyone who disobeys,
to the lions will be cast,
before the sun sets that same day."
(An evil custom of the past.)
This made
the king, Darius, glow,
to think his people
loved him so.
He signed the law
so fast and quick—
He did not see
it was a trick.

But Daniel was a brave old man.
He heard the news
(and saw the plan).
Yet *still* he stopped three times a day
to give thanks to our God, and pray.

Just watch those heartless men
run fast.
"Your Majesty! We just went past
old Daniel's room.
We heard him pray
to his own God, the same old way.
He is the *first* to disobey!"

The king cried out, "Not Daniel!
He's done no wrong. You know it."
"But," these men shout,
"A law is law.
It *must* be kept.
Now show it!"

No help for Daniel.
He's marched then
at sundown to the lions' den.

They push him in.
The lions roar.
The guards clang shut
the heavy door.

The king's in tears,
he's so upset.
He spends the night awake.
"Dear Daniel.
Oh, if he should die,
I think my heart will break."

At dawn, the king then hurries
to the lions' den.
So worried, he can hardly breathe,
he shouts, "Oh, Daniel,
tell me, please.
Could your God save you
from the lions' teeth?"

"Yes," Daniel calls.
"My God shut tight
the lions' mouths
all through the night.
Please don't be sad.
I'm quite all right!"

The king is overcome
with joy.
He makes the guards
let Daniel free.
(The wicked men
are soon destroyed—
thrown in the pit
of snarling beasts.)

To all his people,
far and near,
the king sends out this word:
"Now hear!
Let us praise the God
who has saved Daniel
from the power of the lions.
He works many wonders.
He saves and He rescues.
The God of Daniel is the King
over heaven and earth!"

My, what a celebration then
was held to honor Daniel—
This man who'd faced the lions' den,
so *sure* God could take care of him!

DEAR PARENTS:

The story of Daniel is a story about the "God who works wonders." Which was greater: the amazing rescue of Daniel from the power of the lions or the rescue of Daniel from the fear of both beasts and men?

It was difficult to stay loyal to God and to act upon one's convictions when most people around believed and acted differently. To stay true to God and disobey the law of the land was to face a sure and gruesome death. "But Daniel to his God stayed true," convinced that God was able to save him even out of a lions' den. And, if we may add a thought from another part of the Book of Daniel, even if God did not save him, he would still stay true to Him (Daniel 3:18). Daniel had deep roots in the faith and prayer life of the Jewish community, with its experience of God's faithfulness throughout its history.

Will you help your child see in this story God's marvelous power not only over beasts but also over the hearts of men? And will you help him be nurtured and sustained by the faith of the Christian community, as Daniel was by his? When we know God's faithful love in Jesus Christ we can face even the "lions' den" in trustful obedience to God.

THE EDITOR